AROUND
PERSHORE
IN OLD PHOTOGRAPHS

AROUND
PERSHORE
IN OLD PHOTOGRAPHS

COLLECTED BY

MICHAEL DOWTY

ALAN SUTTON
1988

Alan Sutton Publishing Limited
Brunswick Road · Gloucester

First published 1988

British Library Cataloguing in Publication Data

Dowty, Michael
Around Pershore in old photographs.
1. Hereford and Worcester. Pershore, history
I. Title
942.4'49

ISBN 0-80299-480-2

Typesetting and origination by
Alan Sutton Publishing Limited.
Printed in Great Britain
by WBC Print Limited

INTRODUCTION

During this century's infancy, my grandparents, parents, four aunts and six uncles all lived in Pershore. It was a little before my time, and the town was never my home, but with so many family associations and handed-down memories, it has always seemed the next best thing.

This book's main content is the work of my father, William Ward Dowty 1887–1979, covering the period when he was finding his photographic feet, from roughly 1906–1913. He was born at Pershore on 15 December in the year of Queen Victoria's Golden Jubilee, a year also marked by the arrival of some later notable English names: Henry Bateman, Rupert Brooke, Julian Huxley, Lawrence Lowry, Bernard Montgomery, Edith Sitwell and Barnes Wallis. The following year saw John Dunlop produce the first pneumatic bicycle tyre, whilst George Eastman introduced the Kodak rollfilm camera to the world, with the bright slogan: 'You press the button – we do the rest!'

Life rarely matches its simplifying slogans. Photography, though well-established and rapidly advancing, was still problem-packed at every stage of the process. Perhaps we take our readily available images of the past too much for granted, sparing little thought for the sufferings of those pioneers who lacked today's facilities to help them on their pictorial way. Early illustrations show them encumbered by volumes of clothing and equipment, more in keeping with space exploration than the earthly expeditions from which they would return to darkrooms equally far-removed from any vision of press-button simplicity.

Even when my father entered the family business there was no electricity laid-on, nor was there running water for the washing of plates and prints. His early photographic output may fairly be said to have owed more to Dunlop than to Eastman, for it was the pneumatically-tyred bicycle that enabled him to carry his unwieldy, halfplate reflex camera around the rutted roads and lanes of South Worcestershire. Given less professional aspirations he might have settled for something smaller and simpler, though whether the results would have proved as satisfactory or as lasting is debatable. The glass plate, despite disadvantages of bulk, weight and fragility, yielded negatives of remarkable quality, as demonstrated throughout the following pages.

The photographs are arranged as a simple tour of the area, beginning and ending at Pershore. They were mostly taken for sale as sepia postcards to a largely unsophisticated public, seeking little more than recognisable images of familiar local features. During his modest photographic excursions my father might well have come across that prolific, evocative painter of the English landscape, A.R. Quinton, whose work has been colourfully associated with Salmon postcards since 1912. But Quinton's Wyre and Cropthorne benefit from judicious deletion and addition (take away a chimney-pot or two; add a haycart or flock of sheep) not within the province of honest photography. Whereas the painter included precisely what suited him, the photographer had to make the best of whatever came his way.

In this latter respect there was certainly no shortage of children, magically drawn from cottage and garden, as if the man with a camera were some sort of Pied Piper of Peopleton or Fladbury, or anywhere else. Suddenly becoming models of immobility, they would pose in village street or on five-barred gate as their images were first sharpened on the focussing-screen, then frozen onto a plate. No longer does such magic have the power to draw them away from the box whose screen transmits moving images – 'the electric Cyclops', as a friend once described television.

Unfortunately for purchasers of the original postcards, the children and various other 'pictorial ingredients' were often too minutely reproduced on the small format and consequently got 'swallowed-up'. It therefore seemed a good idea for me to remedy this by revealing some of these hitherto hidden details. In effect it is much the same as 'zooming-in' with a modern camera lens, though with the added advantage of being able to do so retrospectively and at leisure, decades after the event.

My father's Pershore output was considerable, especially when he also found time to sing in the abbey choir, teach at Sunday School and serve in the town's fire brigade (nicely balanced interests – praising God, lecturing on Hellfire and extinguishing earthly flames). The comparatively few surviving negatives (800 or so) are housed at the County Record Office in Worcester, which, in view of their overall weight (as estimated on temperamental bathroom scales) of 160lbs, is perhaps the safest place for them. Although a few are chipped or have suffered in other ways, only one is actually broken – a clean break which you are invited to find, if you can. Incidentally, the equivalent weight of 35mm material would yield in excess of 200,000 negatives, occupying a good deal less storage space.

The 'tour' begins with some family photographs and other relevant material, whilst on the last pages will be found some of my own views of Pershore, taken on what would have been my father's 100th birthday. The 'weight' of content, however, is from the Record Office, and I am grateful to the Head of Record Services, Mr A.M. Wherry, for both his friendly interest and for allowing me easy access to the Dowty Collection, making possible this selection of 'freshened-up' visual memories of a delightful town and its picturesque and friendly neighbours.

Michael Dowty

WILLIAM WARD DOWTY – with camera – in around 1906.

IMPORTANT ADVICE

TO

SPECTACLE WEARERS

It is a fact that

1. More eyes are injured by the injudicious use of glasses than by any other known cause.
2. That a great number of people are wearing Spectacles unsuitable for them and for which their eyes have not been properly tested.
3. That the old-fashioned and unscientific method of testing the eyes trying various spectacles of different strengths until the sight apparently suited, is to say the least of it, dangerous.

Do I need Spectacles?

It is impossible to give an absolute rule which will always indicate the need for Spectacles; but it would be wise to consult a capable Optician:—

When it is necessary to remove print or small objects away from the eye.

When vision is clear for a moment, then suddenly becomes confused and blurred.

When the eyes tire so that it is necessary to close them and rest.

When headaches occur as the result of eye strain.

Points to be noted.

You may walk with an artificial leg;

You may eat and masticate your food by the aid of artificial teeth; but

You cannot see with an artificial eye. Then take care of your eyes, as your sight is invaluable, and if lost can never be replaced.

I test each eye separately and fit the frame to each individual case,

as experience has shown that only by these methods can satisfactory results be obtained.

CALL AND CONSULT

W. DOWTY, Qualified Chemist, Optician, and Photographer,

Grandfather, William Dowty was a chemist, optician and photographer at High Street, Pershore. This is an example of his advertising of optical services in Fearnside and Martin's Pershore Almanac.

PORTRAIT, LANDSCAPE
& ARCHITECTURAL
PHOTOGRAPHER

William Dowty

REMBRANDT HOUSE

High Street

PERSHORE

FURTHER COPIES OF THIS CARTE CAN
ALWAYS BE HAD OR IT CAN BE ENLARGED
TO ANY SIZE & BEAUTIFULLY FINISHED.

The printed back of a mounted photograph.

The only known photograph of grandfather's shop. This copy from a small print shows well-stocked shelves and showcases...

A chair for the customer's comfort, and an un-missable reminder not to neglect the eyes. Ironically, one of his own children, George, lost an eye in boyhood through experimenting with magnesium powder in conjunction with an open fire.

Family group in the garden at 'Rembrandt House'. William and Laura with their eight children who are arranged in order of seniority. From right to left, standing: John, Jessie Maria, Joseph. Seated: William Ward and — far left — Robert. On the ground is Arthur Golding, whilst the twins, Edward Flexton and George Herbert are close to their parents.

W.W.D. at the age of about 24. My mother is likely to have issued an ultimatum on the matter of the moustache, though later — they weren't married until 1917.

The only known contemporary photograph of 'Rembrandt House' – what there is to be seen of it – right of centre, with two bow windows.

The Bank House,
Moseley.
Dec 12th 1887

My dear Mother,

I am pleased to tell you that Wednesday next is fixed for our breaking-up Party, and that you may expect me home for the Christmas Holidays on Saturday morning by the usual Train.

We have had a long Term and I think a very profitable one to most of us for the Report of the Examination shows that the School has done well on the whole.

The Subjects in which most of the boys have excelled are, English History, Geography, Arithmetic, Latin and French.

Four boys were sent to the Examination held by the College of Preceptors and they appear to be quite satisfied with their work. One of our late boys who passed the Oxford Examination with Honours has just taken First Class Honours and a Prize in the Incorporated Law Society's Examination.

During the Term we have had a Giant Stride put-up in the playground for our amusement and and we are promised a Gymnasium very shortly.

We were allowed to go to the Cattle Show this year, which we enjoyed very much indeed; and also went to the Evening Service Moseley Church on Dec 2nd when the New Organ was opened.

Thanking you for past favours and wishing you the Compliments of the Season.

Your loving Son
A. Field.

Three days before my father was born, this immaculate letter was written by a twelve-year-old schoolboy, though it would be unjust to accuse him of being its author. The choice of subject matter and deadly phraseology are strongly indicative of schoolmasterly dictates. Any expression of filial devotion which ends: 'Thanking you for past favours and wishing you the Compliments of the Season. Your loving Son . . .' is bound to arouse suspicion. Frank Field's brother eventually became my other grandfather.

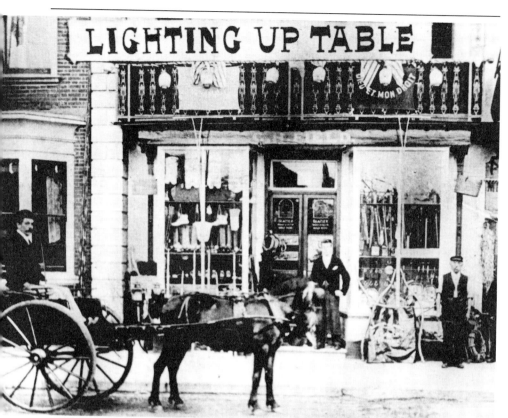

And here is Charlie Field (extreme left) outside his ironmonger's shop at 3, High Street, Pershore. He had four daughters: Evelyn Grace, Dorothy, Winifred and Kathleen, the eldest one being my mother. This memory of grandfather's shop came unexpectedly, many years ago, in the form of a tiny print ($2\frac{1}{2}$ inches $\times$ $1\frac{1}{2}$ inches) sent to my mother by a total stranger who said it had been taken just after the Relief of Mafeking in May 1900. It contains a remarkable amount of detail — cricketing equipment in the left-hand window, agricultural implements in the other, and staff members dutifully posing for the unknown photographer who might have been William Dowty Senior. The significance of 'Lighting Up Table' has never been resolved.

Charlie Field's shop was ideally situated when it came to supplying showmen with oil and other needs at Pershore's Annual Fair, held in Broad Street. My mother and her sisters also had a grandstand view of proceedings. Apparently, all the fair people had to wait at the outskirts of town until midnight struck, and there was then a mad rush to claim pitches.

The wide open tree-lined space of Broad Street as it used to be. Charlie Field's shop is the one on the left, with twin blinds.

Winter sunshine illuminates this bare-tree view of Broad Street. The abbey tower's pinnacles can be seen above the rooftop on the right.

The 'tour' starts here, appropriately enough, for International Stores was almost opposite 'Rembrandt House'. Mouth-watering comestibles at tempting prices (Rich Sultana Cake 6d. lb; Strawberry Jam 6d. & 1s.; Lunch Tongues 2s. per glass) and half a dozen assistants eager to serve.

The name of F. Greenhous was new to me, and only the 'Stictite' poster provided the Pershore location. Closer study of the photograph revealed lettering on the other side of the street, mirrored in the top of the window (left-hand pane), showing the shop to be standing opposite the Angel Inn & Posting House.

Behind the Greenhous glass, only Brasso and Stictite were displayed, representing a highly professional approach to window-dressing.

No helpful reflections to locate the Cheltenham & District Gas Co., though vague shadows suggest it could have been on the east side of High Street.

Unfortunately for the Field girls, the Fire Station was only a few doors away at the top of Bridge Street, and since their father was Brigade Lieutenant they were in effect 'captive cleaners' of the fire engine.

A few yards south of the Fire Station was Central Garage – Cars For Hire; Repairs Promptly Executed. Might there have been complaints about its presence registered on aesthetic grounds?

The top view discloses more of the distant part of the street. The Star Hotel stands beyond the nearside of the parked motor car. The bottom view – from the same photograph – shows what was going on across the street – which wasn't very much. Note the rival garage.

We have moved a little way down Bridge Street and turned around to look back towards the town (and in the lower view, something else has been turned, twice!). We have also turned back the clock, for there is no trace of garages on either side of the street.

A detail from the preceding page. Incidentally, referring to reversed S's, captions had to be written back to front on negatives, which could sometimes lead to confusion.

The rear elevation of 'Stanhope House' in Bridge Street. According to W.W.D. it was the home of a branch of the Sainsbury family. Here is an urgent appeal to any present-day Sainsburys who might by chance see this book: Please resurrect the paper-carrier as soon as possible. It is superior to plastic in all respects – its capacity is greater, it lasts longer, stands rigidly and openly to be filled and doesn't fall-about like an inebriate, spilling its contents on the way home. Thanking you in anticipation.

Leaving the town via Bridge Street, we pass Pershore Mill on our left, and then cross the bridge itself, seen here with its arches all but covered by the Avon in flood.

In this view from west of the bridge, the Avon is at its normal level.

A last look back at the town, from Avonbank, showing how sharply the road bends. To the left of the horse-drawn vehicle (whose driver is smartly top-hatted), the road branches off to Pensham and the Combertons. But we are heading for Wick.

Wick Cross was restored in 1911 and – from the look of it – given a new head.

Composite postcards were popular – a cheap way for the purchaser to send several views for the price of one, even if the quality wasn't much to write home about.

A vintage Wick cottage, whose tattered thatch is in urgent need of attention.

The dovecot at Wick, said to accommodate 1,300 nests.

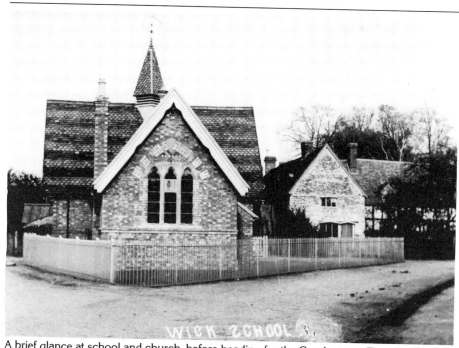

A brief glance at school and church, before heading for the Combertons. The chosen route for the tour is reasonably sane, with the exception of one deliberately introduced complication to test your geographical knowledge of the area.

The rake's retarded progress at Great Comberton. Had it not been for the rake, this view would have been rejected. Very likely, W.W.D. was similarly motivated when he took the photograph.

The unkempt and the 'kempt'. Contrasting cottages at Great Comberton.

Two faces of 'real England'. A pictorially perfect cottage at Great Comberton and Old Farm at Little Comberton, a mile or two away.

OLD FARM LITTLE COMBERTON.

Little Comberton on a day for flinging-open the windows and rolling-up the shirtsleeves.

Berrow's Worcester Journal

——PICTORIAL SUPPLEMENT.——

GRATIS   SATURDAY, JULY 24th, 1909.

Tendon-tensioning toxopholites. A Worcestershire Archery Meeting at Elmley Castle, in July 1909. W.W.D.'s photograph appeared in Berrow's Pictorial Supplement. And since Berrow's newspapers are on target to celebrate their tri-centenary in 1990, might they be persuaded to bring back the supplement?

Elmley actually lost its Norman castle hundreds of years ago. But it has retained its village prettiness without becoming too chocolate-boxy, besides offering easy access to Bredon Hill.

If this rabbit seems troubled, it may be on account of his ill-fitting body, hardly sculpted by the hand responsible for the Savage Memorial in the same church. The Savage family built a manor-house at Elmley in the sixteenth century, and they and their descendants were the occupants until the mid 1800s.

ELMLEY 20

ELMLEY. 8.

Presumably the Savage Manor, classically standing amidst trees and looking out on a generous expanse of lake, complete with swans and cygnets.

'Good Morrow, All. Be mindful of how ye goeth'. The County Police Station at Elmley Castle.

Finally, at Elmley, the Old Mill with its thatch-protected wheel. Possibly the most venerable-looking item in the whole book.

Woollas Hall has stood on the slopes of Bredon since Tudor times. For 400 years it was the seat of the Hanford family, but in recent years it has been divided into apartments.

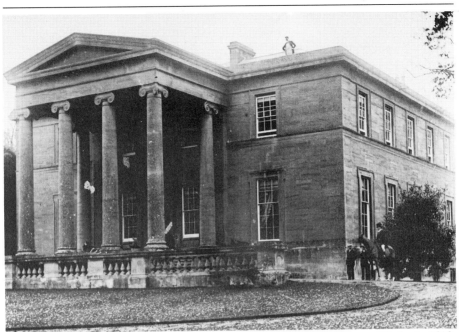

Strensham Court which – in an earlier form – was the birthplace of Samuel Butler in 1612.

Strensham Mill.

Four miles from Strensham was Nafford Mill, mentioned more often by W.W.D. than any of the other mills he photographed. It was destroyed by fire in May 1909, with W.W.D. attending in his official capacity as fireman, and unofficially as photographer. He was fined a punishing 2s. 6d. for 'deserting his post', but as he always maintained that they reached the blaze too late to save the mill, it seemed a bit unreasonable. He probably more than recouped his loss, through reproduction fees.

Detail from the preceding page.

Two further pre-fire views of Nafford Mill.

Moving away from the Avon, we come to Eckington, where a horse is in trouble – it's the nearside fore that's gone.

The old village cross at Eckington crossroads.

The fifteenth-century tower of Eckington Church. The church itself is masked by the adjacent premises of A. Heming, Baker & Confectioner; Corn & Meal Stores.

The church interior which has a wall monument to John Hanford and his wife (Woollas Hall) and to their eight sons and five daughters.

Eckington Station. Only one view, but with a couple of added variations, knowing how railway fanatics love to get close to the subject.

E.J. Simmonds has cornered the Eckington meat market, trading from unpretentious-looking premises. A customer has modestly concealed herself behind the door, whilst he poses with butcher's knife in hand and sharpening steel suspended from his waist.

The General Stores Company pays a painted tribute to Sunlight Soap on its side wall, whilst boosting Nectar Tea and the 'X L' Bakery on metal signs set above the facia.

The absence of thatch in this Eckington street gives it a peculiarly undated look.

The sixteenth-century Eckington Bridge over which we pass, *en route* for Birlingham.

Birlingham's turreted tower is the oldest part of the church which was re-built in the nineteenth century. The tower goes back to the fifteenth century and was also adapted to serve as a dovecot.

When Birlingham's beautifully-sited church was rebuilt, its twelfth-century chancel arch was taken down and re-erected outside, as a gateway.

Birlingham Post Office.

And this, we presume, is the postmistress.

Birlingham School.

A cottage at Defford.

This photograph from the Pictorial Supplement of 9 April 1910, was captioned: 'MARRIAGE OF MISS REVILL (Defford). Photo, Dowty, Pershore'. But what about the groom? Was he of insufficient importance to merit a mention?

Defford Church.

Berrow's Worcester Journal

—— PICTORIAL SUPPLEMENT.——

Gratis | SATURDAY, SEPTEMBER 3rd, 1910.   [Gratis

Photos for Publication must reach us by Tuesday Morning.

The supplement of 3 September 1910, featured the wedding of Lady Dorothy Coventry and Sir Keith Fraser, at Croome. The photographs were taken on the steps of Croome Court.

Croome Court – probably photographed on some other occasion, like a Garden Party. Let's stay on the subject of weddings for a little longer, with W.W.D's recollection of an old local character who had 'seen-off' a couple of wives and went to church to marry his third. When asked to respond to the crucial question: 'Wilt thou take this woman to be thy lawful wedded wife?' he did so, positively: 'Ah, that I will, if she'll be as good to me as she has been this last foortnit!' On another occasion, when we were shown W.W.D.'s cine-film of a big 'Society Wedding' (nearly always the worst to photograph), we remarked on the rakeishness of the bridegroom. 'I should say he was', said W.W.D. 'When the wedding was all over, he ran off with the chief bridesmaid!'

Appropriately close to Croome Court is what has always been known as Dunstall Castle and generally accepted as having been the 'folly' of the very capable Lancelot Brown, designer of the estate grounds at Croome, and responsible for the planning of Kew Gardens. Dunstall has been referred to as: 'the ruins of a castle', in which case – as the photograph shows – they must be some of the tidiest ruins to be found anywhere.

Pirton Church contains both Norman and Tudor work (its timbered tower is currently being restored). This is not, perhaps, one of W.W.D.'s better photographs, but – if the clock is to be believed – the time was 7.05 a.m., and the shadows and other clues suggest it was an autumn morning, lovely to be out on, but not the best time for this particular subject.

Boxbush Farm, Stoulton. Today, the same photograph would be taken from the forecourt of Stoulton Motor House, and would be of Boxbush Cottages.

The Rainbow Fair at Stoulton School on 26 June 1913. (By this time, W.W.D. had bought his own business at Worcester). The Guest of Honour has been presented with the customary bouquet, and everyone is delighted by the occasion's charm and grace.

A mile or so down the Pershore Road from Stoulton is the Plough and Harrow – 'By L. Sandbrook; British and Foreign Spirits' says the sign – and it looks like a big day for the twin daughters of the house who are showing-off a brace of new bicycles.

This further detail from the previous page shows – presumably – Plough and Harrow staff members sharing in the joy of the occasion.

Here, we have a mystery. The wording on this establishment is unreadable, and one can only presume it to have been in Stonebow Road, Drakes Broughton (half a mile or so from the Plough and Harrow).

The whereabouts of Mr William Ewins' business is similarly impossible to pinpoint. All we know is that he was a 'Licenced Dealer in Tobacco; Grocer and Provision Merchant'.

Turning left at the bottom of Stonebow Road, Drakes Broughton, we arrive – after two or three miles – at Spetchley. Spetchley Park has been the home of the Berkeleys for more than three centuries. These may well be family members, relaxing with their dogs.

Cattle at Spetchley Park.

Taking the Stratford Road from Spetchley, the first place we come to is Broughton Hackett, where an elderly lady surveys her cottage garden. Have you ever wondered how people in those days managed to keep their lawns shorn and control the weeds?

Upton Snodsbury comes next. The vicarage in Pershore Road looks directly onto St Kenelm's Church.

Other properties in Pershore Road, Upton Snodsbury, photographed from somewhere near the vicarage gate.

Shoeing at Snodsbury: 'You 'old on to 'is 'ead, and I'll 'ammer 'is 'oof!'

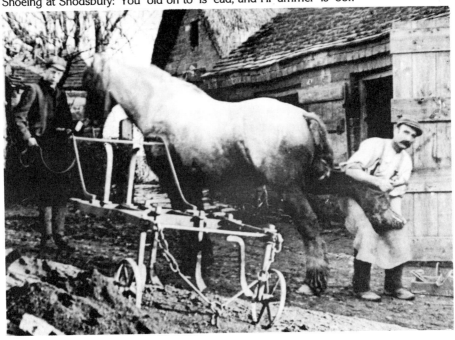

Grafton Flyford Mill stands right by the Stratford Road, a few miles on. (It is still there today.)

Nearby Dormston has one of the county's most notable dovecots, with accommodation for more than 700 nests.

The church at Flyford Flavell has an especially rural setting, even to the extent of a duckpond – a hint of which is in the foreground.

Moving south of the Stratford Road, we first come to a pleasing country cluster at Abberton.

The tower and spire of Abberton Church. (The spire has long since been removed – it was a potential danger to low-flying aircraft.)

Rous Lench Court. The house and seven acres of terraced grounds combine to provide what is perhaps the finest Tudor survival in the county.

The Norman south door of Rous Lench Church. Here, the doormat is both novel and informative, for it leaves the visitor in no doubt as to the direction of his arrival, by simply stating: 'South Door'.

The interior of Rous Lench Church.

A detail from above the chancel arch in Church Lench Church.

At Bishampton we stop for long enough to ponder the fate of this sad little cottage. Today's parlance would refer to it as 'being in need of some renovation'.

Throckmorton Church tower looks down on better cared-for cottage thatch.

These farm cottages at Throckmorton are also fairly respectable, though some of the brickwork is a little ragged.

Peopleton Church is another of those with a pretty setting, though it differs from some of the others we have seen by having a modern tower (nineteenth century) tacked on to a building whose walls date from the thirteenth century.

The main road through Peopleton. Children have obligingly appeared and will be rewarded by being featured more prominently in the section below.

Peopleton Mill.

The Crown Inn, Peopleton. The landlord is Alfred Loxley – that must be him in the foreground, hiding beneath a capacious cap.

Here is an extremely rutted road at Pinvin, near Pershore.

It is not yet time to return to Pershore, and we now head in the direction of Evesham, passing over the pretty little bridge leading into Wyre Piddle.

Polite society more usually refers to Wyre Piddle as 'Wyre'. But no matter what you choose to call it, it is easy to see the appeal it had for any painter or photographer. Wyre, as it was then, had almost a surfeit of visual charm. Today, many of the charming cottages have disappeared, and the place has an altogether tidier aspect.

A.R. Quinton painted this near-identical view of Wyre Cross and the main street, looking towards Evesham – with one or two artistically-licensed amendments.

Another batch of children willingly facing the camera. It is interesting to note the greater daring of the Wyre girls. Another point to ponder is the absence of footpaths in Wyre and all the villages in this book, with the exception of Eckington.

Not a soul in sight in this peaceful afternoon view of Wyre. Even the horse has been removed from the shafts of the delivery van belonging to the bakers and grocers, J. Derrett & Sons.

A pair of postmen by Wyre Cross.

Finally, at Wyre, signs of life speeding-up. Why, there might come a time when even postmen ride effortlessly on four wheels instead of having to exert themselves on two.

Carrying-on towards Evesham and past Fladbury crossroads, we come to Woodnorton, seat of the Duke of Orleans in the days before the BBC had been invented. King George V is due to pass through the Golden Gates (October 1910), which explains the policeman's guarding presence.

The Golden Gates at Woodnorton.

Having referred to Evesham a time or two, we might as well have a brief look at it, especially as it was the birthplace of William & Laura Dowty. William was the son of John Goddard Dowty, a wheelwright of Bengeworth, whilst Laura was one of the 14 children of Joseph Masters, three times Mayor, a well-known market gardener and staunch enough an advocate of temperance to earn himself the nickname of 'Coffee Masters'. In this photograph of High Street, every vehicle is horse-drawn, except the prominent automobile, parked – we regret to note – on the pavement.

Evesham Rowing Club's boathouse at Crown Meadow. Less tolerant club members might have poured scorn on the form of transport shown overleaf.

A pleasure steamer moored near Evesham Bridge. A Dowty photograph in the Berrow's Supplement of 3 July 1909, is captioned: 'First Steamer Excursion on Avon at Pershore', though whether 'first' referred to first ever or first of season is not clear.

Evesham Bridge. Perhaps I am not alone in thinking of it as the 'Workman Bridge', for a commemorative tablet refers to it having been built through 'the public spirit and perseverance' of Henry Workman. The bridge was completed in 1856, its predecessor having been similar to the bridges at Pershore and Eckington.

Two sections from the preceding photograph. We are looking in the direction of Bridge Street, though virtually nothing of it can be seen, owing to the foreground activity. The man approaching us has a large delivery basket on his arm, and heading in the opposite direction behind him is another man with a large rake over his shoulder. There is a suggestion of trouble about to break-out with two of the three children on the left — though who could possibly say what happened next? Lastly, on the extreme right (and therefore on the wrong side of the road) is a baker's van embarking on its round from Port Street.

Here, a small boy takes a lively interest in the activities of workmen who have removed the globe from one of the bridge lamps. But two of the men have discovered the camera looking at them and are consequently attempting some sort of visual trick for posterity.

Leaving Evesham by the Worcester road, we come to The New Inn at Cropthorne, though standing, as it does, on the main road it hardly seems a part of the village. Anyway, it is a family hotel, providing teas for motorists and cyclists, and it also has a 'Private Room'.

If the New Inn looked a little jaded (it appears rather spruce today), we find the village itself quite up to the mark and picturesquely peaceful. Not even the 'thatched frown' of the nearer cottage can detract from the tranquility of this view.

Resolving this Cropthorne mystery is beyond me. Perhaps someone else will be able to shed some light on the subject. Is it a chapel trying to be a barn, or a barn with religious mania?

Being located on a hill enhances Cropthorne's charm. This is another view to have caught Quinton's eye, though in his rendering the sign for L. Meakins, Grocer has been re-sited, and one or two other deviations from the truth achieved.

Here is where the road sharply falls out of sight, arousing speculation as to what lies beyond. And wasn't it extraordinarily civil of this young chap to pose with his bike, especially with the irresistible prospect of such a super hill to scorch down?

On second thoughts – after a closer look – maybe his bike isn't best suited for scorching, and there is a pretty sharp bend at the bottom.

Cropthorne Post Office, as pretty an example as you will find anywhere, and worthy of a couple of closer looks.

In its original sepia postcard form, this photograph would have been bought and as likely as not posted here, then carried by the very same postman on the first stage of its journey. What an added novelty to the sending of a simple picture postcard.

Perspective and viewpoint change the picture, which is of the same post office, but with the emphasis placed on its nearer neighbour. The postman, of course, has departed on his round.

Cropthorne Mill.

The Avon, near Cropthorne.

Fishing party. A scene and variations at Cropthorne Mill.

Next, to Charlton, whose post office doesn't really rival Cropthorne's for charm, though everyone seems anxious to oblige the photographer, including the postmaster – it must be him – on the left, the postman and several children.

Another clutch of Charlton children, backed by a sumptuous assortment of summer shrubs and hedges.

Fladbury, the penultimate village of the tour, is linked to Cropthorne and Charlton by a bridge built to commemorate Queen Victoria's Golden Jubilee. Fladbury Church – in terms of age – has something in common with Cropthorne. Visually – certainly when photographed from this particular angle – it is not the prettiest-looking ecclesiastical edifice.

An ivy-dominated view of the lower end of Fladbury, where the road drops down to the meadows flanking the Avon.

Although it is similar to the previous view, this was taken at a later date and from higher up the road. You may be able to see that someone has decided to do something about the ivy problem on the furthest building. A barely visible horse and cart makes its slow, uphill way round the corner – to judge from the state of the carriageway, it is a fairly busy road.

Three Fladbury children on a sunlit, five-barred gate. And now we shall go up to Fladbury crossroads, turn left and visit Moor.

Moor Post Office is one of the most detailed photographs in this selection, with the enlarged window area on the facing page being especially 'dressed' with interest.

In the two preceding prints, the window was hardly detectable; now, its contents are readable. The name of Esther Bullock appears above the window, and we are told she is a 'Provision Dealer' and also a 'Licensed Dealer in Tobacco'. As to the window itself, it contains penny packets of table jelly, Colman's Starch (plenty of that), Quaker Oats, B.D.V. Cigarettes, Jacob's Biscuits (penny packets), Cadbury's Cocoa Essence, Provost Nuts, Crawford's Biscuits (also in penny packets), and Player's Cigarettes. Hours of business – Post Office, that is – are listed in the top centre pane.

More children at Moor.

A more mature Moor family group, with dog. We shall now return to Pershore, via Wyre and turning left at Pinvin crossroads.

E. Humphries & Co. (Atlas Works) are across the road from Pershore Station. In this view from the north-east they advertise themselves as 'Engine & Thrashing Machine Works', rather than the more usual 'threshing machine'.

The east end of the Atlas Works.

Pershore Station somewhere around 1910. Amazingly, when I photographed it in 1970 when its demolition was imminent, remarkably little had changed, apart from the departure of the gas lamps. So, from the time the passenger footbridge was erected in 1901, the station stayed clear of trendy innovations until the sledgehammer arrived to knock it into today's shape of an offensively cheerless bus stop.

A train is arriving at the London platform, awaited by a group of elegantly feminine passengers.

For the fanatics, here is a closer view of the locomotive, and I can tell you that its number — only faintly legible on the buffer-beam — is 3682. Unfortunately, all the books in my own modest railway collection insist on 3682 being an 0-6-0 pannier tank. Well, at least we know something they don't know.

We mustn't leave the station without acknowledging the signalbox with three GWR servants in close attendance.

Back into town to complete the tour. We are in Worcester Road, looking towards High Street. The pony and trap facing us (if you can see it) belongs to G. Lane, Pershore Dairy, whilst a few yards beyond it is the Plough Inn. Further away still, on the opposite side of the road, is the Chequers Inn.

Looking back in the direction from which we have just arrived. This time the Chequers Inn is in the left-hand foreground.

This is a sight many of us can remember growing-up with – the coal cart, drawn by a quietly efficient, good-natured horse. This one, probably photographed in Worcester Road, is J. & N. Nadin's, whose address was – not surprisingly – Pershore Station.

The location of this and one or two of the following views is not at all clear. They are almost certainly of roads in the vicinity of the abbey. Perhaps it would be wise to follow an old rule: 'If you have nothing to say – don't say it'.

This one was captioned: 'The Old Lodging House'.

This is definitely Newlands, hardly – at that time – the most salubrious-looking of Pershore's thoroughfares. Nevertheless, it was – according to W.W.D. and other members of the family – the childhood home of a well-known romantic novelist, whose work has long proved a boon to both her publishers and her starry-eyed readers.

The negative from which these prints were made is suffering from a most peculiar disease, giving it the appearance of having been packed in honeycomb. Not that it seriously detracts from the overall charm of the photograph.

On the other hand, the volume of ivy clinging to St Andrew's tower does detract from its architecture, almost to the point of obscuring it. We might even be looking at a high-rise swarm of bees. Today, of course, it is clean-shaven.

Two interiors of Pershore Abbey.

The White Horse Hotel in Church Street.

St Andrew's Road has several nasty potholes in it, and altogether looks in need of urgent care and attention. Its present-day face is infinitely healthier, proving that progress can really mean progress.

Pershore Cottage Hospital has had – like any other hospital – its share of triumph and defeat in matters of life and death. Charlie Field died there on 29 May 1911, aged 43. The following extracts from his obituary and report of the funeral provide something of a word picture of the times, and mention of many contemporaries who shared them.

(C. H. Field obituary and funeral report extracts.)

SUDDEN DEATH OF MR. C. H. FIELD. The death of Mr. Charles Henry Field, of Broad Street,* which took place at Pershore Cottage Hospital at two o'clock on Monday afternoon, after less than a day's severe illness, came as a real shock to the townspeople, and indeed to the whole district round, for he was one of the best known men in the locality. Mr. Field was seized with intense internal pains on Sunday night, and it was found he was suffering from peritonitis of a most violent and unusual description. He was at once removed to the Cottage Hospital, and Dr. Gosling, of Worcester, assisted by the local doctors, performed an operation. The grave apprehension which from the first was entertained for his recovery was unfortunately realised and he passed away as stated. All day Saturday, and till late in the evening, deceased was pursuing the ordinary duties of his business, and the many who saw him and heard his cheerful conversation then find it hard indeed to realise that he now lies cold in death. Unexpected as is the sad event, it appears that Mr. Field had suffered some little time from the complaint to which he ultimately succumbed, and had been obliged to seek medical advice. But it did not interfere with his getting about or with the performance of his everyday duties, and only one or two were acquainted with the fact that this genial, breezy, good-hearted personality was affected by so grave a disorder. These characteristic traits mentioned had much to do with making Mr. Field so popular and so welcome, everywhere. Few social gatherings took place in Pershore at which he was not present, and no one had prior authority to sing the old hunting song "John Peel", for no one could produce Peel's "whoop-a-loo" anything like he.

"But now he is gone, far, far away,
We shall ne'er hear his voice in the morning."

These lines, sung by deceased hundreds of times, will recur with painful meaning to so many who have heard them from his lips over and over again. Deceased and his family have been connected with Pershore for a good many years. His late father was a Warwickshire man, and his mother is a native of Pensham, being sister to Mr. J. E. Bullock, the well-known vocalist. Mr. Field was apprenticed to the late Mr. Walter Pace, ironmonger, Broad Street,* who was also the local manager of Lloyd's Bank, and it was when the bank was removed to its present position some eighteen years ago that Mr. Field succeeded to the premises and business. Deceased married the only daughter of the late Mr. William Smith, builder, of Pershore, and she with four daughters now mourn his death. Deceased's brother, Mr. Frank Field is a well-known cricketer, and is fast bowler for Warwickshire. Deceased had but recently been appointed on St. Andrew's Parish Council, and judging by the meeting he attended last month would have proved a very useful and outspoken member. He had been a member of the Pershore Fire Brigade, ever since its re-formation twenty years ago, and for most of that period served as lieutenant. He was for many years a sidesman of Holy Cross Church, and at a public meeting held the other week he was elected a member of the committee arranging the Coronation festivities. Deceased was quite a sportsmen; in his youth he was a keen participator in all the games, and up to the last was an enthusiastic follower of the Croome Hunt. The deepest sympathy is felt for his wife and daughters in their great and irreparable loss.

The funeral took place at the cemetery on Wednesday afternoon, and notwithstanding the unusually short notice, a large number was present to pay their last tribute of respect to his memory. It was a day of brilliant sunshine, and long before the arrival of the cortege many were present at the cemetery which is kept in perfect condition. The whole service was impressively conducted by the vicar (the Rev. F. R. Lawson). Following the hearse were three coaches containing Messrs. Frank Field (Warwick) and J. Field (Watford), brothers, G. Farmer, F. Aston, H. Smith, J. W. Smith, W. G. Y. Pitcher, D. Workman and J. Mytton. Next in the procession came six members of the Pershore Fire Brigade in their uniform and burnished helmets – viz., Messrs. W. L. Wright, C. Wright, E. T. Nutting, W. Dowty, jun., J. Edwards and G. Daniels. The procession also included The Rev. J. Dolphin, Messrs. F. Nicholas, H. Nicholas, W. Dowty, T. Guest (postmaster), F. Greenhous, W. Wood, W. Taylor, A. E. Baker, W. H. Knight, C. Yorke, H. Watts, W. A. Beach, P. J. Prothero, G. Phillips, F. Allsopp, E. T. Grizzell, W. T. Chapman, P. Hanson, J. W. Smith, C. E. Ballinger, R. Hook, W. Nicholas, F. Nicholas, J. Dowty, J. Sherwood and others. The bearers were Messrs. G. Dolphin, S. Annis, G. Taylor and S. Grinnell. The plain oak coffin, with brass furniture, made by Mr. J. W. Smith, bore the inscription: "Charles Henry Field, died May 29th, 1911, aged 43 years".

* Both references should surely have been to High Street.

Pershore High Street.

Pershore High Street.

On the facing page is Pershore's Working Men's Club (still there today, without the railings), scene of an ingenious practical joke played by Arthur Baker, a 'lively' local solicitor. He went into Grandfather Dowty's shop and asked if he might have an empty medicine bottle with a blank-label, and a sheet of brown paper in which to wrap it. Grandfather duly obliged, and Mr Baker wrote on the label, wrapped the bottle and then deposited the package outside in the gutter. Presently, up the street came the team of roadmen, making their customary slow progress and led by Emmanuel Jones who was also a lay preacher. Spotting the package, Mr Jones stooped and picked it up, addressing his team in his best declamatory tones as he did so: 'Ho, Boys! This is h'evidently something of h'importance. Let us therefore adjourn to the Working Men's Club and see what it containeth!' Once inside the club, the package was carefully unwrapped, revealing the empty bottle on whose label Arthur Baker had written: 'Roadman's Sweat, worth a guinea a drop'.

I previously related this story in some notes written for the Pershore Millennium in 1972, and incurred the displeasure of one of Mr Jones' relatives who said I would never have used the story had I known what a good man he had been. In defence, I can only say that good men are no more immune to practical jokes than bad men. For all I know, there may be someone at this very moment writing a label with my profession on it – though I sincerely hope not, for I am typing this at 3.15 a.m. and have absolutely no intention of going outside to track stray packages. (Actually, it is 3.19 a.m.)

The Working Men's Club.

Here's another one from Berrow's Supplement. On the face of it, a typical group of English gentlemen, but there are imposters in its midst, for the caption reads: 'Japanese Deputation to Pershore Fruit Market'. This took place in October 1910.

This might appeal to anyone with a passion for old cars. Located immediately behind the bonnet is something closely resembling an outsize press-stud.

Ernie Payne was a highly feared competitor at local events. He carried-off so many trophies that – according to W.W.D. – other cyclists eventually 'ganged-up' on him in an attempt to curb the winning streak. He is seen here being push-started at Pershore Flower Show.

GUSTAV HAMEL AT PERSHORE. OCT. 22

In October 1913, Gustav Hamel paid – literally – a flying visit to Pershore. It was he who made the first official Airmail flight in this country, carrying mail from Hendon to Windsor in September 1911. But no one has yet explained what brought him to Pershore.

GUSTAV HAMEL AT PERSHORE OCT. 23. 1913.

Hamel's visit seems a fitting enough way to conclude this selection, for, as already mentioned, W.W.D. had, in effect, 'taken-off' for Worcester, though for a time he did have family matters to cope with at Pershore.

The remaining pages contain my own photographs, taken as a personal record of Pershore, seen on the 100th anniversary of my father's birth.

But first, here is the broken negative – the Bridge at Wyre Piddle. And if you are still unsure about the error in the tour's route, Strensham was out of place, resulting in either considerably more mileage or the need to change into some dry clothes. I do hope you didn't find the course too exhausting.

Pershore. 15 December 1987.
The International Stores has been updated to Gateway Foodmarkets.

Christmas trees for sale in High Street, £4.25.

The Post Office yard in the era of the four-wheeled postman.

The kiosk by the car-park exit. Let's hope British Telecom (what a silly, ugly name for a company) will leave it there.

The old Fire Station, pleasantly transformed and now known as 'Belle House'.

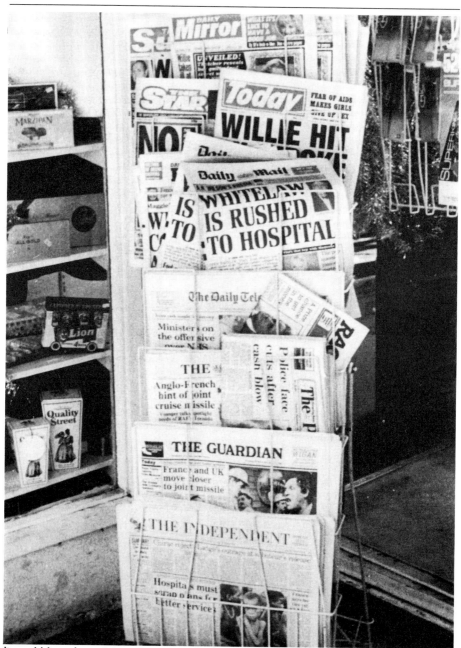

It would have been interesting to see the headlines of 15 December 1887. Today's cover Lord Whitelaw being rushed to hospital, trouble – as always – in the NHS, a possibility of France and UK producing joint Cruise missile and right at the time when M. Chirac is defending his right to release saboteurs. Help!

Pre-Christmas pedestrians in Broad Street.

Broad Street. No longer the wide open space.

The many-fingered post at the top of Broad Street, and Charlie Field's old shop (still an ironmonger's) in the background.

The old Field shop, sandwiched between its neighbouring dispensers of money and pharmaceutical products.

Last of all, the birthplace of William Ward Dowty (15 December 1887), and therefore the birthplace of this book. Today, the property is occupied by Savory & Moore, the Chemists.